CAN'T I JUST DO SOMETHING For Me?

How Hobbies Heal, Help, and Remind You Who You Are

Jennifer Larsen

Printed in the United States of America

ISBN: 978-1-968756-78-9

First Edition

Cover design by Rachel Bostwick

Interior design and layout by Rachel Bostwick

For information or bulk orders, visit cantijust.com

Contents

▣ Introduction:
This Isn't a Self-Help Book. It's a Wake-Up Call from the Fun Police.

At some point, you stopped liking things.

Not because you stopped being curious or joyful or weird in all the best ways — but because life got heavy. And somewhere in that heaviness, you quietly set down the stuff that used to make you feel alive.

Not because it was wrong. But because it wasn't *required*.

You grew up. You got a job, a mortgage, maybe a kid or two. You filled your calendar with obligations and called it a life. Somewhere between "should" and "have to," joy got repackaged as something optional. Or childish. Or selfish.

And now here you are — burnt out, bored, or wondering if your best years happened back when you were still making questionable art with glitter glue.

If you've said any of the following lately, this book is for you:

- "I used to have hobbies... I just don't have time anymore."

- "I wouldn't even know where to start."

- "Everything I like turns into work."

- "I don't even know what I enjoy anymore."

You're not lazy. You're not boring. You're not broken.

You're just overdue to do something **for you** – not for money, not for clout, not for productivity points. Something that makes your brain light up. Something that makes time pass in the best way. Something that reminds you what it feels like to be *you*.

This book isn't about becoming an expert or launching a side hustle. It's about making space in your life to try things, suck at them, and love them anyway. Each chapter has a simple exercise or reflection to help you reconnect with what matters – not because you *have* to, but because you *get* to.

So no, this isn't a self-help book.

It's a map back to joy.

And you don't even need to color inside the lines.

▦ Chapter One:
Whatever Happened to Just Doing Stuff for Fun?

You used to love things.

Not because they were useful. Not because they were impressive. Not because they earned you likes or money or status.

You just liked them.

You wrote fanfiction. You doodled during class. You messed around with Legos or guitar chords or cake decorating or cosplay or comic books. You stayed up late reading for fun, not because a reading app told you to.

Then something changed.

Adulthood came in hot with its bills and expectations and soul-sucking schedules. Somewhere between trying to be "successful" and trying to keep everything from falling apart, you got the message – spoken or not – that joy was optional.

Optional if you could afford it.

Optional if you had time.

Optional if you'd finished your to-do list (you hadn't).

Optional if you were good at it.

Optional if you could monetize it later.

Before you knew it, all the things that used to make you feel *you* got labeled "extra." Extra time. Extra energy. Extra money.

And if you didn't have those? Well, too bad.

But here's the thing: the stuff we do "just for fun" isn't extra. It's *essential.*

It's how we know who we are — separate from our jobs, our families, our messes. It's how we regulate stress, build confidence, meet people, and give our brains a break. Fun isn't fluff. It's function.

And right now, a lot of people are starving for it.

Exercise: The Flashback Five

Let's take it back for a second.

List five things you used to enjoy doing before adulthood convinced you that joy was a luxury:

1.
_____

2.
_____

3.
_____

4.
_____

5.
_____

Circle one.

Now imagine trying it again – just once. No expectations. No pressure. No performance. Just… trying.

- What would it feel like to revisit it?

- What's stopping you?

- What if you gave yourself one hour, this week, to see what comes up?

Reflection: What Did You Notice?

Write a few sentences. No rules. Just jot it down.

What stood out as you listed those five things?

Did one make you smile? Miss something?

What used to feel possible that doesn't anymore – and why?

◯ Why This Matters

You weren't wrong to like the things you liked.

You just got busy. Tired. Distracted. Responsible.

But joy doesn't stop being important just because you have car payments and a calendar full of obligations. In fact, that's when you need it most.

This isn't about reclaiming childhood.

It's about reclaiming *yourself.*

➡ Up Next: You're Not Lazy — You're Starved for Joy

Let's talk about what really drains you — and why hobbies refill more than just your schedule.

Chapter Two:
You're Not Lazy –
You're Starved for Joy

Let's just say it out loud:

Most people who think they're lazy are actually **exhausted**.

Not just physically tired (though, yeah, that too). But emotionally tired. Mentally drained. Spiritually zapped. The kind of tired that doesn't go away with sleep because it comes from living a life with **too many demands** and **not enough delight**.

You've been managing bills, appointments, kids, parents, jobs, crises, dishes, paperwork, bad news, and group texts for years. Of course you're tired. Of course fun feels impossible. But that doesn't mean you're lazy. It means you've forgotten what *fills* you instead of drains you.

▶ Here's the problem:

When joy disappears, your body and brain still need something to regulate stress and give you a sense of aliveness. So you start reaching for quick-fix replacements:

- **Doomscrolling**
- **Binge-watching shows you don't even like**
- **Numbing out with snacks, drinks, apps, noise**
- **Online shopping spirals at 2am**
- **Just... zoning out** for hours, doing nothing in particular

None of those make you bad. They make you human. But they also make you more tired, not less. Because they don't actually recharge you – they just distract you.

This is where hobbies come in. Actual ones. Creative ones. Weird ones. Pointless, joyful ones.

Hobbies don't drain your energy – they **return** it.

They give you a sense of choice in a world where most of your day is dictated by other people's needs. They reconnect you with curiosity, flow, creativity, and surprise. They're the mental equivalent of getting a deep breath after holding it for hours.

And unlike doomscrolling, they don't leave you feeling worse afterward.

🌱 Exercise: The Energy Audit

Take a piece of paper and draw a line down the middle.

On the left, write **DRAINS ME**.

On the right, write **FILLS ME**.

Now go through your typical week. Write down everything you do – big or small – and try to sort it into one column or the other.

✦ Examples:

- Work meetings? → Drains me

- Walking the dog in the morning? → Fills me

- Laundry? → Drains me

- Playing music on the way to work? → Fills me

- Scrolling for an hour? → ...Trick question. Might feel neu-tral, but usually leaves you dull.

Take a good look at those lists.

Where could you swap a 15-minute drain for a 15-minute fill?

Reflection: What's One Small Shift You Can Make?

You don't have to overhaul your life. But you can reclaim little slivers of it.

What's one thing from the **"Fills Me"** side you want more of this week?

What's one thing from the **"Drains Me"** side you might replace – even once?

Write a sentence or two to anchor your intention.

◯ Why This Matters

You're not failing. You're fried.

You don't need to push harder. You need something that **pulls** you – back into yourself, back into joy, back into the part of you that still wants things.

The world doesn't make it easy. But that's why this matters so much.

Joy isn't a reward you earn.

It's a resource you need.

➡️ You Don't Need a Thing – You Need a Spark

Forget passion. We'll start with curiosity – and see where it leads.

Chapter Three:
You Don't Need a Thing –
You Need a Spark

Quick question:

What's your thing?

No seriously – what's your *thing*?

Cooking? Photography? Gardening? Slam poetry? Rock climbing? Woodworking? Yoga? Dungeons & Dragons? Restoring vintage typewriters?

...No?

If your brain just went blank or panicky, you're not alone.

Somewhere along the way, we started believing that every fully-formed adult should have a "thing" – a hobby, a passion, a quirky obsession they can casually drop into conversation like:

"Oh, I'm really into vintage guitars and black-and-white film photography. I roast my own beans, too."

Meanwhile, you're sitting there thinking:

I sometimes rewatch the same show for comfort and panic-purchase notebooks I never use. Does that count?

Yes. It does.

Because here's the truth: **you don't need a "thing."** You just need a **spark**.

A flicker of curiosity. A glimmer of "what if?" A weird little urge to try something *for no reason*.

That's where it starts.

Passions aren't born – they're *built*. One small, uncertain, possibly awkward step at a time.

👀 The Myth of the Fully Formed Hobbyist

We think everyone else knows what they're doing. That the painter friend was always good at art. That the hiker coworker always loved nature. That the person knitting on the train somehow *knew* at age six they were born to purl.

Wrong.

Most people just tried something. Got mediocre at it. Laughed at themselves. Kept going.

Your "thing" doesn't arrive fully assembled.

It gets pieced together from scraps of curiosity you were brave enough to follow.

You don't need talent.

You don't need a plan.

You just need to notice what makes you lean forward and go, *"Huh... maybe."*

🔍 Exercise: The "Maybe" List

Take five minutes. No judgment. No overthinking.

Write down **at least five things** you've ever thought looked cool or interesting — even if you've never tried them, and even if they scare you a little.

1.

   _____

2.

   _____

3.

   _____

4.

   _____

5.

   _____

Now go back and put a ⭐ next to the one that feels the **least intimidating** to try first.

It doesn't have to be free. Or convenient. Or make any sense.

It just has to be... interesting.

You're not marrying it. You're just flirting with it.

◯ Reflection: What's Holding You Back?

Look at the list again.

- What came up emotionally?

- Did you write down something you used to like and for-got about?

- Did you immediately start judging yourself for what's "re-alistic"?

Write 1–2 sentences about what you want to try and what's been getting in your way.

⬭ Why This Matters

The pressure to "have a thing" keeps people from trying any-thing.

But identity doesn't come from waiting for clarity.

It comes from *doing stuff* – especially when you're not sure how it'll go.

You don't need to be certain. You just need to be **interested**.

That's the spark.

Let's build from there.

⏩ Up Next: Scroll, Work, Sleep, Repeat

We're about to break the consumption cycle – and invite your brain back into creation, play, and real presence.

Chapter Four:
Scroll, Work, Sleep, Repeat

Let's talk about the cycle.

You know the one.

Wake up tired. Work. Manage chaos. Crash on the couch. Start scrolling. Maybe binge something. Maybe open and close five different apps without doing anything at all. Feel like you wasted the night. Go to bed late. Wake up tired again.

Scroll.

Work.

Sleep.

Repeat.

You're not alone. You're also not broken.

You're stuck in a **consumption loop** – and it's one of the most common symptoms of burnout, boredom, and emotional depletion.

Because when your energy is low and your brain is tired, it doesn't crave stimulation – it craves *escape*. And apps are *really* good at offering that.

No judgment here. This isn't an anti-phone, anti-TV, anti-TikTok rant. This is a reminder that your brain **wants more** than just watching other people live their lives.

At some point, you stopped creating.

Stopped playing.

Stopped engaging with the world through your own hands, your own ideas, your own curiosity.

But you didn't stop *wanting* to.

You just forgot how to start again.

🎨 Creating Isn't Just for "Creative People"

We've been tricked into thinking that only "creative types" are allowed to make things.

That painting is for artists. Music is for musicians. Writing is for writers. Everything else? For watching.

But creating is a human need – not a personality type.

Whether you're building a table, baking muffins, making a playlist, planting a window herb box, designing stickers, fixing a lawn mower, or rearranging your living room furniture in a fit of impulse – it all counts.

Creation is anything that turns **you** into the source instead of the spectator.

And when you shift into creator mode, something changes. Time moves differently. You breathe differently. Your brain lights up. You're *present* again.

That's what hobbies give back to you.

📺 Exercise: Content Audit

Let's see what your days really look like from a "doing vs watching" perspective.

For the next 24 hours, keep track of what you watch, scroll, or passively consume.

- TV shows

- YouTube

- Podcasts

- TikTok/Instagram

- News articles

- Reddit

- Anything that doesn't require input from you

Now go back and ask:

Did anything I consumed make me want to try something?

Mark those items with a ✦.

It could be small. Like:

"That cooking video made me want to bake banana bread."

"That art reel made me want to pick up my old sketchbook."

"That travel vlog made me want to go outside."

That's the line. The one between watching and doing.

Reflection: What Crosses the Line?

Pick one thing that gave you even the smallest spark of curiosity.

What would it take to **cross the line** and actually *try* it yourself?

Time? Confidence? Supplies? Permission?

Now write a sentence or two about how you might start. Just start. No results required.

Why This Matters

Passive consumption isn't evil – but it's not nourishment.

And when you're only consuming and never creating, your sense of agency shrinks. You feel duller. More reactive. Less *you*.

Creation – even small, silly, imperfect creation – **wakes you up**.

It reminds you that you're not just a set of eyeballs attached to a tired body. You're a maker. A builder. A player. A doer.

Even trying once counts.

And hey... if you mess it up? Good. We're going there next.

➡️ Up Next: It's Okay to Suck at First

We're going to lovingly destroy perfectionism and invite your inner chaos goblin to make some ugly art with us. 🐱 🎨

Chapter Five:
It's Okay to Suck at First

Let's get one thing straight:

You are not supposed to be good at new things.

That's the deal. That's the price of admission. That's the magic of it.

And yet, somehow, we've convinced ourselves that if we're not instantly amazing at something – if we're awkward, slow, unco-ordinated, or wildly mediocre – it must not be "our thing."

Which is like giving a toddler a violin and saying, *"Ugh, I guess you're just not musical."*

No. They're just new.

And so are you.

☀ Perfectionism Is Killing Your Joy

Let's be real: most people don't quit hobbies because they're too busy. They quit because they're too uncomfortable being bad at something.

They feel clumsy, embarrassed, out of sync with the version of themselves that's supposed to be competent and capable. Adults don't like looking like beginners.

But here's the truth: **every joyful thing in your life started with you being bad at it**.

You didn't come out walking. You toddled and fell.

You didn't start school already knowing how to write your name.

You didn't learn to cook without burning stuff.

You didn't start your job already knowing how to juggle twelve Slack threads while eating a sandwich over your keyboard.

You *learned*. You practiced. You sucked for a while — and then didn't.

That's how it works.

Your Inner Beginner Is Still Alive

That part of you that's willing to be a mess, to play, to experiment, to look silly? It's still in there.

Buried under years of adulting and self-doubt, sure. But it's not gone.

It's just waiting for you to stop demanding instant results.

Because hobbies aren't about mastery. They're about *process*. Presence. Play. Mess.

And most of the time, the worse you are at something, the more you laugh. The more you experiment. The more you actually engage.

What if the thing you're bad at is the thing that saves you?

Exercise: The Ugly Art Challenge

You ready for this?

Create something awful on purpose.

Yep. That's the challenge.

- Draw the worst portrait of yourself imaginable.

- Write a terrible poem about soup.

- Build something ridiculous out of whatever's on your desk.

- Record yourself singing off-key about your grocery list.

- Make a hideous craft out of recycling bin trash.

Just. Make. Something. Bad.

Then answer this:

- What felt fun?

- What felt weird or awkward?

- Did anything surprise you?

- Would you do it again?

You are officially invited to fail gloriously.

Reflection: What Are You Afraid Will Happen?

Now write down what usually stops you from trying new things.

Embarrassment?

Feeling wasteful?

Fear of judgment?

Not being good fast enough?

Then answer honestly: *Is that fear serving you? Or is it just keeping you stuck?*

◯ Why This Matters

Trying and sucking is better than not trying at all.

Because sucking leads to play. Play leads to presence. Presence leads to joy. And joy brings you back to life.

If you're waiting to be good at something before you start, you'll never start.

So go be bad at something. Be ridiculous. Be a beginner.

Your future self will thank you for not waiting until it was perfect.

■ Up Next: Try Stuff Without Stressing Out

No spreadsheets. No guilt. No five-year plan. Just one experiment at a time. You in?

Chapter Six:
Try Stuff Without Stressing Out

Let's cut the drama.

Trying a new hobby doesn't have to mean reorganizing your whole life, buying $300 worth of supplies, and committing to it for the rest of eternity.

You don't need a schedule. Or a plan. Or an accountability buddy with a Google calendar invite.

You just need **three tries**.

Three no-pressure, low-stakes attempts. That's it.

Because here's what happens when you turn curiosity into obligation:

- It stops being fun.
- It starts feeling like another job.
- You start resenting the thing you *wanted* to enjoy.

So let's skip the self-sabotage and go simple.

Try something. Three times. With the lightest heart possible.

🎯 The 3-Try Rule

Most things feel weird the first time.

- You're self-conscious.

- You don't know what you're doing.

- You feel like everyone else has a secret manual you weren't given.

But the second time? It feels… a little better.

And the third? You actually know what to expect.

That's why three tries matters.

It's long enough to get past the awkward start, but short enough that it doesn't feel like a big commitment.

After three tries, you'll know:

- Do I enjoy this?

- Do I want more of it?

- Or was this just not for me (and that's okay)?

You don't have to marry the hobby. You're just going on a couple dates.

Exercise: The 3-Try Test

Pick **one small hobby** from your "Maybe" List (or anything you've been curious about lately).

Then set a goal: try it **three times**, for **30 minutes or less** each time.

Use this tracker:

Try #	What You Did	How It Felt
1		
2		
3		

You don't need to be good. You don't need to impress anyone.

Just notice how it feels – physically, emotionally, mentally.

What's different between Try #1 and Try #3?

Reflection: What Got Easier?

Think back on your three tries.

What shifted between the first and third attempt?

What surprised you – good or bad?

Did your confidence grow, even a little?

Write a few thoughts. (And if you didn't get to all three yet, write what you *expect* might happen.)

💬 Why This Matters

The hardest part of anything is starting. The second hardest part is sticking around long enough to know if it's worth it.

Three tries gives your brain a chance to move from panic to play.

You're not building a resume. You're not signing a contract. You're just seeing what fits.

Sometimes it clicks. Sometimes it flops. Both are wins.

Because you showed up for yourself.

Without pressure. Without guilt. Without performance.

And that's what this whole thing is about.

➡️ Up Next: Find Time, Not Perfection

You don't need more hours in the day. You need to reclaim a few of them for yourself – and I'll show you how.

Chapter Seven:
Find Time, Not Perfection

So let's get this out of the way first:

You *do* have time.

Not *always*. Not *a lot*. But somewhere in that mess of work, worry, and whatever's on Netflix, there's a little slice of time that could be yours again.

It's not that you're lazy. Or unmotivated. Or incapable of "sticking to things." You're just... tired. And used to putting yourself last.

But hobbies aren't luxuries. They're lifelines.

And they don't need two uninterrupted hours, a pristine desk, or total silence to happen. They just need **a small window where you reclaim your attention**.

Where Time Is Hiding

The good news? You probably don't need to overhaul your schedule. You just need to notice where your energy and attention are quietly leaking away.

Here's where time usually hides:

- The **20-minute scroll** before bed
- The **"I'm too tired to move" couch collapse**
- The **15 minutes early** you get to school pickup or an appointment
- The **show you're watching but not really watching**
- The **long checkout line** you're standing in, eyes glazed over

No shade. Truly. Your brain is doing what it knows to do when it's tired: defaulting to low-effort loops.

But what if – even once this week – you reached for something fun instead of something mindless?

You don't need a productivity app. You need a tiny, joyful interruption.

⏰ Exercise: Time Swap

Let's run a little swap experiment.

1. **List three things** you regularly do that take time, even just a few minutes:

A.

_____

B.

_____

C.

_____

2. Now ask:

- Could I replace one of these *just once* this week?

- Could I *reduce* it by 10 minutes and use that time for something fun?

Examples:

- Scroll for 30 minutes → Paint for 10, then scroll guilt-free

- Watch 3 episodes → Watch 2, crochet during one

- Sit in the car waiting → Read, sketch, knit, plan, dream

Don't kill the habits. Just... carve a little space out of them.

🪷 Reflection: When Does Joy Fit Best?

Write down the part of your day when you feel *most like yourself*.
Not most productive – most *you*.

Is it:

- Right after the kids go to bed?

- While you're sipping coffee?

- Sitting in your car after a long day?

What would it take to protect 15 minutes of that time for some-thing fun?

💬 Why This Matters

You don't need to be perfect. You need to be *present*.

You don't need a whole afternoon. You need a corner of it.

Most people wait for big, open windows of time that never come. But hobbies don't live in wide open spaces – they live in the margins.

Steal back your minutes.

Sneak in your joy.

Give yourself the first slice of the day, not the scraps.

➡️ Up Next: When People Don't Get It

We're gonna talk about other people's confusion, judgment, and unsolicited opinions – and how to protect your joy anyway. 🖤 🖤

Chapter Eight:
When People Don't Get It

You finally start doing something fun for yourself.

You're feeling a little spark again. A little flow. A little you.

And then someone ruins it.

"That's what you're doing with your free time?"

"Huh. That's... different."

"You know there's no money in that, right?"

"Wow, you must have *a lot* of time on your hands."

Cool. Thanks for the energy, Janet.

Other people's discomfort has a funny way of showing up when you start doing something joyful and unapologetically yours.

Sometimes it's confusion. Sometimes it's judgment. Sometimes it's subtle mockery disguised as teasing. Whatever the form, the message is the same:

"Why are you doing that if it's not useful, impressive, or profitable?"

Here's the answer:

Because it makes me happy.

And that's enough.

⋈ Why People Push Back

It's not always about you. (In fact, it's *almost never* about you.)

When someone mocks or minimizes your hobby, it's usually because:

- They're uncomfortable with doing something "just for fun."
- They were never given permission to play themselves.
- They feel insecure about how *they* spend their time.
- They think rest = laziness and fun = wasted potential.
- They forgot what joy feels like and resent you for remembering.

That doesn't excuse it. But it helps you stop absorbing it.

Other people don't need to get it. They don't need to "approve" your joy. They don't even need to understand it.

They just need to stay in their lane.

And you need to stay in your light.

Exercise: Build Your Hobby Shield

Let's build a quick emotional response plan – something you can say, out loud or just in your head, when someone tries to shrink your joy.

Fill in these blanks:

"It makes me feel _____."

"I do it because _____."

"I don't need to be good at it. I just need to _____."

"This matters to me because _____."

You don't have to recite this to anyone.

It's for *you*. A little internal armor.

And if you *do* need an out-loud answer for an annoying comment?

Try one of these:

- "Because it makes me happy."
- "Not everything has to be useful."
- "I like it. That's reason enough."
- "Because I can. 😊 "
- "It's more fun than judging other people's hobbies."

Pick your tone – playful, proud, deflective, savage. You do you.

🪷 Reflection: Whose Voice Are You Hearing?

When you hesitate to try something new – or feel silly for doing something you love – stop and ask:

Whose voice is that?

A parent? A partner? A friend? A coworker?

Or just your inner critic, wearing someone else's old voice?

Write it down. Then rewrite it.

"You're wasting your time" → "This *is* my time."

"That's not useful" → "Joy *is* useful."

"You're not even good at that" → "And yet I'm allowed to love it."

💬 Why This Matters

Joy is personal.

Fun is not a group decision.

Other people's approval is nice – but it's not required.

Protecting your hobbies is *self-respect in action*.

Not because the hobby matters to them – but because *you* matter to you.

So let them raise their eyebrows. Let them make their comments.

You've got better things to do. Like beadwork. Or watercolor. Or writing terrible songs about soup.

Your joy doesn't need a panel of judges.

It just needs you to keep showing up.

➡️ Up Next: It Doesn't Have to Be Productive

We're about to destroy the side hustle trap and remind you: not everything has to earn. Some things just have to *exist*.

Chapter Nine:
It Doesn't Have to Be Productive

Let me say it as clearly as I can:

You are allowed to do things that do not make money.

You are allowed to do things that do not scale.

You are allowed to do things that never become content.

Not everything has to be a side hustle.

Not everything has to be shared.

Not everything has to *matter* to anyone but you.

You can bake a cake and not post it.

You can paint a picture and throw it away.

You can take a class and never use the skill again.

You can make a thing just to make it.

That's not waste. That's freedom.

💼 The Side Hustle Trap

We live in a world that has trained us to monetize everything:

- You crochet? You should open an Etsy shop.

- You love writing? Start a Substack!

- You enjoy photography? Freelance it.

- You make good soup? You should totally launch a meal prep business!

Listen. There's *nothing* wrong with turning a hobby into something bigger – *if that's what you want*.

But the second you feel pressured to turn joy into income, the whole vibe changes:

- Fun becomes output.

- Curiosity becomes performance.

- Play becomes pressure.

Suddenly, your relaxing hobby now has deadlines, inventory, engagement stats, and taxes.

Sometimes that's awesome. But sometimes it **kills the joy you were trying to revive**.

So here's your official permission slip:

You don't have to make money off your joy.

You don't have to share it.

You don't have to explain it.

You just get to enjoy it.

🔹 Exercise: Would I Still Do This If...

Answer honestly.

- If I never got paid for this, would I still do it?

- If no one ever saw it, would it still matter to me?

- If I wasn't "good" at it by any standard, would I still want to try?

Now flip it:

- Have I *not* tried something because I couldn't picture it going somewhere?

- Have I talked myself out of joy because it "wasn't worth the time"?

Write a few sentences about what that reveals.

Reflection: What's the Real Reward?

Forget money, followers, or external praise.

When you imagine yourself doing this hobby in private – just you, no audience, no pressure – what's the emotional reward?

Calm?

Confidence?

Control?

Connection?

Curiosity?

Comfort?

Name it. Claim it. That's your "return on investment."

Why This Matters

You're allowed to do things badly, privately, and just for you.

That doesn't make them frivolous.

That makes them **sacred**.

We don't need more influencers.

We need more people who are quietly, stubbornly joyful.

So if the only purpose of your hobby is that it makes you smile, helps you breathe, or gives you something to look forward to?

That's not wasted time.

That's a life well lived.

➡️ Up Next: Let It Be Just for You

We're going to talk about sacred space – how to protect, preserve, and savor the joy you're building without letting it get co-opted by guilt or outside pressure.

▨ Chapter Ten:
Let It Be Just for You

You've found something that brings you joy.

It's small, maybe. Quiet. Unimpressive to the outside world.

But it's yours.

And now comes the hard part:

Can you let it stay yours... without turning it into something for everyone else?

It's tempting. Once you like something, your brain starts buzzing:

- "Should I make an Instagram account for this?"
- "Maybe I could sell this eventually..."
- "I should invite other people to do it with me."
- "Would this look good on a résumé?"

STOP. BREATHE. SMILE.

You don't have to turn your joy into a project.

You're allowed to keep this one thing **just for you**.

🔒 Sacred, Small, and Secret (If You Want)

Think about how many things in your life are shared, tracked, or optimized.

- Your schedule is shared.

- Your time is scheduled.

- Your energy is spent on other people's needs.

- Your accomplishments are measured.

- Your fun is often public (or it didn't "count").

So when you stumble across something that lights you up? Don't rush to share it.

Let it be weird. Quiet. Private. Messy. Half-finished. Undocumented.

Let it be the one thing in your life that doesn't have to *become* anything.

You deserve a joy that doesn't get filtered through someone else's expectations.

🎙️ Exercise: Claim Your Space

Write this out, in your own words:

"I give myself permission to have joy that is _____, _____, and _____."

"I don't owe anyone _____."

"This hobby doesn't have to become _____ to be valuable."

"It matters because _____."

Hang this somewhere. Read it when your guilt flares up. Or when someone asks, "So what are you going to *do* with that?"

You're already doing something.

You're reclaiming space for yourself.

Reflection: What Parts of Your Life Feel Fully Yours?

Seriously. Pause here.

What do you have in your life that no one else controls, judges, or schedules?

If the answer is "nothing"... that's not failure. That's information. That's a gentle red flag waving at you, saying:

"Make room."

Even one hour a week. One corner of your home. One playlist. One notebook. One moment in the day that's *yours*.

It doesn't have to be big. It just has to be **real**.

💬 Why This Matters

We're trained to perform everything.

Even our rest. Even our fun.

We turn everything into content, currency, or competition.

But you're allowed to have a part of your life that's just yours.

No audience. No angle. No return on investment.

You're allowed to exist for yourself.

And if that feels radical? That's because it is.

➡️ Up Next: When It Becomes Something More

We're heading into the final chapter – where we gently acknowledge that *sometimes*, these little sparks grow into something bigger. And that's okay too... *if* it comes from joy.

Chapter Eleven:
When It Becomes
Something More

Here's the twist:

Sometimes, the thing you do *just for fun*...

Turns into something more.

Not because you planned it. Not because you forced it.

But because joy, when nurtured, has a funny way of expanding.

That silly project you started in secret?

Turns into a blog, a podcast, a book, a class.

That weekly sketching practice?

Turns into an art show or a side income.

That weird skill you learned on a whim?

Turns into a career change or a new identity entirely.

And when that happens – when your fun thing becomes your real thing – it can be amazing.

But the key? **It has to come from love, not pressure.**

🌱 Let Joy Lead

If your hobby grows, let it grow on *your terms*.

Not because someone else said you should.

Not because you feel guilty for "wasting time."

Not because hustle culture got in your head.

Let it grow because it *wants* to.

When joy leads, effort feels like momentum – not pressure.

When curiosity leads, learning feels like play – not work.

When *you* lead, everything else can follow.

You don't owe anyone progress.

But if progress shows up? Let it feel like a gift.

🔁 Exercise: From Fun to Future

Think of something you're doing (or considering) that started as "just for fun."

Now answer these:

1. What would it look like if this stayed small and joyful forever?

2. What would it look like if it grew naturally into something more?

3. What's one small sign it might want to grow? (Ex: a friend asked to learn from you, someone offered to buy your work, you keep thinking about it.)

Now ask:

Am I still enjoying this?

Do I *want* it to grow?

If so – what would "growth on my terms" look like?

🌣 Reflection: Joy, Not Judgment

Write this out:

"If this becomes more, I want it to feel _____."

"If I start taking this seriously, I promise not to _____."

"Even if it turns into something big, I'll protect the part of it that's _____."

Growth can be beautiful – when it's chosen.

Make that choice from inside yourself, not from outside noise.

💬 Why This Matters

Not everything has to grow. But *some* things want to.

And when that happens, you get to choose:

- To nurture it
- To protect it
- To scale it
- Or to keep it exactly where it is

You're not starting a business. You're following joy.

You're not launching a brand. You're staying curious.

And if it turns into something bigger?

You'll be ready.

Because you've built it from the most solid foundation there is:

Fun. Play. Curiosity. You.

Up Next: Closing – Your Joy Deserves Space

 **Closing:
Your Joy Deserves Space**

You've made it to the end.

Not the end of your hobby journey – not even close. But the end of the part where you need permission.

You don't need it anymore.

You've got the spark.

You've got the tools.

You've got the right to want *more* than work and worry and waiting for the weekend.

Your life is not meant to be just survival.

Your time is not just for obligation.

Your energy is not just for everyone else.

You are allowed to want things.

To try things.

To suck at things.

To love things that make no sense to anyone but you.

Joy is not a reward.

It's a right.

And you've got it.

So go pick up the weird little hobby.

Buy the supplies. Start the project.

Protect your time. Ignore the judgment.

Play. Make. Try. Quit. Try again.

Let your joy be sacred. Let it be messy. Let it be yours.

You don't need a finish line.

You just need a starting place.

And this?

This is it.

Final Exercise: Your Hobby Promise

Write your own permission slip. Just a sentence or two. Make it yours.

"This week, I give myself permission to try _____, even if I'm not good at it.

I want to do it because _____."

No one else needs to see it.

But if you write it down, your brain will remember:

You matter.

Your joy matters.

You don't need a reason to love something.

You just get to love it anyway.

CAN'T I JUST WANT SOMETHING

For Me?

👤 About the Author

Jennifer Larsen writes books that help people get unstuck – emotionally, practically, and creatively. She's the founder of Wayfinder Press and the Wayfinder Foundation, and she believes hobbies aren't just hobbies – they're how we heal, grow, and remember who we are. When she's not writing, she's probably building something quietly joyful that no one else will ever see. And that's kind of the point.

📄 About the Wayfinder Foundation

Wayfinder Foundation Inc. helps people of all ages explore careers, build life skills, and reconnect with who they are. Through free books, workshops, and school outreach programs, Wayfinder supports those who are navigating change – whether they're just starting out or starting over.

Learn more at wayfinderfoundationinc.org

Explore more books at cantijust.com

Other Books You Might Like

From the "Can't I Just..." Series:

Can't I Just Do Something for Me? is part of the "Can't I Just...?" series, including:

- *Can't I Just Stay in My Room?* (Career guide for teens)
- *Can't I Just Skip College?* (Alternatives to traditional college)
- *Can't I Just Help My Kid Pick a Path?* (Parent guide to the career books)
- *Can't I Just Be Like Everyone Else?* (Teen soft skills)
- *Can't I Just Hit Reset?* (Forgiveness for kids)
- *Can't I Just Get It Together?* (Adult soft skills)
- *Can't I Just Do Something for Me?* (Adult hobbies) ← *you're here*

www.ingramcontent.com/pod-product-compliance
Lightning Source LLC
Chambersburg PA
CBHW051322120626
46547CB00015B/2345